Growing Herbs
As
Aromatics

Growing Herbs As Aromatics

by Roy Genders

Illustrated by Linda Diggins

Keats Publishing, Inc. New Canaan, Connecticut

GROWING HERBS AS AROMATICS

Published in 1977 by Keats Publishing, Inc.
by arrangement with Darton, Longman and Todd, Ltd.
London, England

Copyright © 1977 by Roy Genders
All illustrative material © 1977
by Darton, Longman and Todd, Ltd.
All Rights Reserved

ISBN: 0-87983-155-3
Library of Congress Catalog Card Number 77-865-44

Printed in the United States of America

Keats Publishing, Inc.
36 Grove Street, New Canaan, Connecticut 06840

Contents

Contents — contd.

Part III: Further practical information

PART ONE

History of Aromatics

1. AROMATICS IN EARLIER TIMES

Since man first appeared on earth, aromatics (plants with fragrant properties) have been a part of his existence. Early man must have been aware of the preservative properties of aromatics as well as of their value for flavouring food and drink. The cooling properties of trees and shrubs with scented foliage were also of importance to those who inhabited the warmer parts.

The ancient Egyptians were the first people to show an appreciation of aromatics, but the records of the highly developed civilisations of the Ancient World tell us that their peoples were all familiar with the use of spices and of fragrant herbs. Aromatics were widely used by the citizens of Greece and Rome; the Bible contains very frequent references to aromatics, for, as with many of the people of ancient times, these played a large part in the religious as well as the everyday life of the Hebrews. The Koran speaks of them; and, as far back as we can trace them, aromatics have been of significance and use to the peoples of India, China and Africa. It could be said that, wherever aromatics grow, man has made use of them and taken pleasure in them.

Aromatic herbs were known in Britain from early times. By the Middle Ages their cultivation and use was highly developed; aromatics were an essential of life to all classes of people. To look at the use of aromatics at this period is not only interesting but illuminating; many of the ideas and practices of the times could well be adapted for our pleasure and benefit today.

Sweet Flag – *Acorus calamus*
(Also called Sweet Rush and sometimes *Calamus aromaticus*)
All parts of this plant have a delicious cinnamon-like scent. It is
found wild in various parts, especially in ditches, the margins
of lakes and marshy places. It was used in Medieval times as a
strewing herb.

2. THE MIDDLE AGES: AROMATICS IN THE HOUSE

Strewn on floors

During mediaeval times scented flowers and herbs were used for strewing on the floor of church and manor to combat the unpleasant mustiness caused by damp earthen floors and lack of windows. There is a record of a payment made as early as 1226 for '12d. for Rushes for the Baron's chamber' and, in 1516, for 'flowers and rushes for chambers for Henry VIII'.

Much in demand for strewing was the scented rush, *Acorus calamus*, which was used to cover the floor and pews of churches as well as the stone floors of houses of the wealthy – it was expensive. It was also known as the cinnamon iris for, when crushed, it gives off the same aromatic scent as cinnamon.

The sweet-scented rush is a plant native to Britain, as well as to other parts of Europe and the East. From the long narrow leaves, which resemble those of the water iris, a volatile oil is distilled which is an ingredient of perfumery and is used for making aromatic vinegars; whilst the root, dried and powdered, makes a refreshing talcum powder.

Calamus root is an ingredient of one of the most popular perfumes of the modern world, Chypre.

Green rushes formed a cool and pleasant 'carpet' in church and home, but had the fault of attracting fleas and other insects, and it was necessary to burn fleabane

(Erigeron) at regular intervals. This plant was usually to be found growing in marshy places with the rushes.

Aromatic herbs, too, were widely grown for strewing, especially those which released their fragrance when trodden upon; germander and hyssop, for example, which Parkinson said were much used for the purpose, 'being pretty and sweet'.

It was Thomas Tusser, an Essex man, who gave the most practical instruction on gardening at the time. He published his *Five Hundred Points of Good Husbandry* in 1573.

Amongst twenty-one aromatic plants he recommended for strewing, and which released their refreshing perfume when trodden upon were basil and balm; chamomile and costmary; lavender and hyssop; sage and thyme. Surprisingly he makes no mention of meadowsweet, which Elizabeth I preferred on the floor of her apartments.

A visitor to this country in 1560 had this to say of an English home: '... The neat cleanliness, the exquisite fineness, the pleasant and delightful furniture ... wonderfully rejoiced me; their chambers and parlours strewed over with sweet herbs, refreshed me.' And he also made mention of the 'sundry sorts of fragrant plants' used about the house, including pots of rosemary, and lavender hung on the wall.

There was good reason for this; it has quite recently been proved that aromatic herbs have a cooling effect on the air. Therefore, although he arrived at his recommendation by other than scientific deductions, Sir Hugh Platt, the Elizabethan, suggested that 'in summer, the chimney fireplace be trimmed with a bank of fresh moss and at either end have a rosemary pot'.

At a later period, dried lavender and rosemary was strew over the rush matting used to cover stone floors;

when walked upon, they released their aromatic perfume. And the strewing of aromatic herbs played an important part on ceremonial occasions. For example, at the time of the accession of James II, one Mary Cowle was 'Strewer of Herbs in Ordinary to His Majesty' and in Huish's History of the Coronation of George IV there is a detailed account of the Herb Strewer and her functions.

Fumigation using aromatics

Apart from their use for strewing on floors, aromatic herbs were used in many other ways in rooms from early mediaeval times on, and to the same purpose; to offset the smells of damp and poor sanitation. One way of perfuming a room was to burn seeds and fragrant woods on open fires, and, in his *Calendar for Gardening* (1661), Stevenson suggested that 'one should be sure night and morning to perfume the house with angelica seeds, burnt in a fire-pan or chafing dish of coales'.

Dr Turner has given in his *Herbal* (1551) several ways of scenting a house. One was to burn southernwood on a low fire when it would not only release its deliciously pungent smoke but would also 'drive away serpents lurking in corners' – frogs and toads which may have entered a downstairs room in summer to find the cool damp floor to their liking during warm weather.

In England in Tudor times, servants were employed at the big houses for the sole purpose of fumigating apartments. Professional perfumers also travelled the country, calling at the homes of the rich, to carry out the fumigation of rooms, but poorer people were not denied the pleasure of aromatic scents in their rooms. 'Nard' was the countryman's name for *Inula conyza*, Ploughman's

Spikenard, and its dried roots were burned, for they gave off a smell like that of spikenard and on many a cottage fire the roots were used together with logs of the sweet scented apple.

Mary Eales, Confectioner to Queen Anne, in her *Book of Receipts* (1682) gives a way of scenting a musty room. It is to take three spoonfuls of dried and powdered rosemary and as much sugar as to fill half a walnut (a delightful way of measuring) beaten into a powder. Then scatter into a perfume pan over hot embers and soon the room will be filled with a delicious perfume. Queen Anne particularly loved the smell of rosemary.

This is a pleasing way of scenting a room, but not all rooms today have the luxury of an open fire. However, a room may be easily and pleasantly scented by burning dried lavender stems.

Scented waters and polishes

In Elizabethan times, it was also a common practice to sprinkle rose and other fragrant waters on the floors of apartments whenever necessary. A cheap scented water would usually be used, possibly made from the roots of native plants which were readily available about the countryside. One of these was *Sedum rhodiola*, known as Roseroot, since its roots yield the fragrance of the rose. It grew in every cottage garden and on old walls and cliffs.

Another delightful practice in Tudor homes was to use scented leaves to give lustre and fragrance to furniture. The seeds of sweet cicely pounded in a mortar, then rubbed on to oak floors and furniture, would impart a myrrh-like perfume and a glossy finish, whilst the aromatic juice from the leaves and stems of balm, *Melissa officinalis*, to be found in hedgerows about the country-side, would impart a polish and lemon-like perfume when used in a similar way.

Pot-pourris

During Elizabethan times, every house, humble or grand, was fragrant with the delightful odours of pot-pourris, a method of counteracting the smell of dampness in use since mediaeval times, when aromatic herbs were gathered from the countryside to be dried and placed in muslin bags to hang from the low-beamed ceilings.

Many recipes for pot-pourris have been preserved. Here is one: Queen Henrietta Maria, daughter of Henry IV of France and wife of Charles I, made up her favourite moist pot-pourri to this formula. A 6 in. layer of fragrant red or pink rose petals is placed in an earthenware jar, covered with salt and allowed to settle for several days before adding to it another 6 in. layer of rose petals, some orange blossom (*Philadelphus*, 'mock orange', will do), some clove-scented pinks, lavender flowers and rosemary. Add another layer of salt, some powdered orange or lemon skin, a sprinkling of dried marjoram and a quarter ounce of powdered cloves. Keep the jar tightly closed until entering a room, then remove the cover and release the delicious perfume, closing it again when leaving the room.

3. THE DISTILLATION OF AROMATICS IN THE MIDDLE AGES

The distillation of flowers and leaves was one of the tasks in all large houses from the beginning of the sixteenth century. The household books (1502) of the Fifth Earl of Northumberland contain the names of 'herbes to stylle', to make sweet waters to use for personal cleanliness, in cooking and for medicine. Balm and sage, marigold and tansy were amongst the most widely grown plants for distillation, and every garden had its rosemary and lavender bushes. All large houses possessed a room for the drying of herbs and another for their distillation, where the ladies took lessons in the art of making aromatic waters.

The commercial distillation of lavender began early in the seventeenth century. Mitcham in Surrey, England, is the home of lavender growing, and its climate and soil produce the world's finest lavender water. It is, however, not from the actual flowers that the oil is obtained but from the tiny green bracts which enclose them. The lavender is harvested in August and September, when it is cut with a sickle as it always has been, and placed on mats for conveying to the still-house.

The earliest recipe for English lavender water is from a manuscript of 1615 which directs that the flowers be distilled with canella bark, wallflowers and grains of paradise; the distillate could be taken internally as well as being used as a perfume for toilet water. Lavender water was the favourite scent of Queen Henrietta Maria, and of Nell Gwyn.

The English firm of Yardley have for years been noted for their lavender products. George Yardley was one of the first settlers in Virginia. Early in the nineteenth century his descendant William Yardley began distilling lavender in water to market a product which quickly came to be used by men and women alike.

Balm was one of the chief ingredients of the celebrated Carmelite Water, made at the Abbey of St Juste. Carmelite Water was used as an elixir for many purposes, both inwardly and outwardly. It was made from two pounds of balm leaves; a quarter pound of lemon peel, two ounces each of nutmeg, cloves and coriander seed, the bark of cinnamon and angelica root; to which was added 'a half gallon of orange flower water and one gallon of alcohol'. It was allowed to stand for several weeks before placing in a still, then slowly distilled to make a gallon of the celebrated water – it was then ready to use; taken inwardly, inhaled, used in baths and as a toilet water. Hungary water was similar to Carmelite water, and was used in the same way.

These and other aromatic distillations were used from early times as toilet water. From the beginning of the eighteenth century, following numerous outbreaks of the plague, scented baths became popular. Personal cleanliness was at last beginning to be recognized and aromatic herbs placed in a warm bath gave the water not only a delicious fragrance but helped to relax tired limbs.

A hand water for use at table was one of the refinements of a more enlightened age. Rose water was placed on the dining table for washing and perfuming the hands. In all wealthy men's houses, silver bowls were kept in the bedrooms and were filled with lavender or rose water to be used for washing the hands and face and to sprinkle over clothes.

4. AROMATICS ABOUT THE PERSON

The care of clothes

From earliest times, scented leaves were placed amongst clothes and sheets and were carried about one's person to combat personal odours, for there were not the opportunities for maintaining the body in the same degree of cleanliness as there are today. Lavender, rosemary and southernwood were grown for this purpose, sprigs being dried and placed between linen and clothes.

Sachet powders were popular with Elizabethan housekeepers, to place amongst clothes and to keep away moths. The violet scent of orris root was much in demand, also the dried leaves of such aromatics as mint and thyme, rosemary and lavender. Sir Hugh Platt made a sweet scented powder by pounding and mixing together the roots of orris and calamus, together with some cloves, storax, lavender and rose petals; it would retain its perfume for a year or more. It can be made in the same way today.

Where possible, clothes were placed around a fire which was releasing the fragrance of a perfume pan, for there was no dry cleaning in those days, and it was necessary to impart a fragrance to clothes to counteract body odours. The clothes were placed around the fire at night when retiring to bed and by morning the garments would be pleasantly scented. Sheets were perfumed in the same way.

Cassolettes and pomanders

We have noted the extensive use of distilled aromatics as
toilet waters. There were other ways in which people of
earlier times were able, by using aromatics, to carry a
sweet scent around with them.

The 'cassolette' or 'printanier' was a popular device for
diffusing aromatics and was introduced towards the end
of the sixteenth century. In the British Museum there is a
manuscript containing a recipe for 'a paste for a cassolette' made to the requirements of Charles II's queen,
Catherine, Duchess of Braganza. It suggests mixing together two drachms each of ambergris, musk and civet,
to which is added a little oil of cloves and three drachms
of essence of citron. The whole should be made into a
paste with lavender or rose water and placed in the cassolette, a small box made of ivory, silver or gold, its lid
perforated with holes through which the scent of the
paste could be inhaled.

Pomanders first came to be used in France, possibly as a
protection against the plague. Henry V, victor of Agin-
court, carried with him 'a musk ball of gold' which he
may have obtained during his French campaign. This was
a ball of musk-smelling amber (pomme d'ambre), which
was later replaced by dried oranges stuck with cloves, like
the one which Cardinal Wolsey carried with him on his
visiting days, tied to his belt.

Elizabeth I usually carried with her a pomander made
in the shape of a ball composed of ambergris and benzoin.
Later, pomanders were made of silver or gold and worn as
a pendant to a lady's girdle. They were constructed in
sections, each one to be filled with a different perfume.

An earlier type of pomander was perforated with small
holes. These were filled with sweetly scented herbs and
could be suspended by a cord from the ceiling.

Scent Containers of Former Times
From left to right: Chatelaine Vinaigrette – Acorn-shaped
perfume flask, English, early 19th century – Silver Flacon,
Dutch or German, 1890.

5. THE MEDICINAL PROPERTIES
OF AROMATICS

Aromatic herbs were not only valued for their delightful scent and their uses about the house. During the seventeenth century when the plague ravaged England, aromatics were used to camouflage the unpleasant body smells of those who were struck down, to disinfect the sickroom, and to help ward off the pestilence. Medical practitioners of the time carried at the end of their walking stick a cassolette filled with aromatics which they held to the nose when visiting the sick. A medical writer of the time suggested burning benzoin, storax, aromatic roots and scented woods.

At the time of the Great Plague (1665), the Deanery of old St Paul's, which was destroyed in the Fire of London the following year, was fumigated twice weekly with aromatics whilst angelica root, dried and powdered and steeped in vinegar was placed in a pan over hot embers and clothes and church vestments hung around at night.

Rue was also in demand to keep away fleas and bugs which were rightly supposed to be the cause of so many diseases. It was one of a number of herbs, rich in essential oil, which the disease-carrying bugs would not go near, used to combat the Black Death and later, the plagues.

Later, in 1750, rue was used to strew the dock of the Central Criminal Court at the Old Bailey as a guard against jail fever which at that time was raging in

Newgate Prison, and the custom continued until the present century.

Much more recent research has proved that aromatics do indeed destroy some bacteria. Early in the 19th century, the Pasteur Institute in Paris, discovered that the micro-organisms of yellow fever were quickly killed by the essential oil of cinnamon and thyme, also by angelica and sandalwood, the bacteria being disposed of in less than an hour and in some cases, within a few minutes.

From his experiments on the bactericidal properties of essential oils conducted a few years later, Prof. Omeltschenki proved that the typhoid bacillus was destroyed within forty-five minutes in air containing the vapour of oil of cinnamon and that tuberculosus bacilli were destroyed within twelve hours of exposure to the vapour of oil of lavender. So that there is a medical reason for those visiting the sick to keep in their handbag or pocket a handkerchief sprinkled with lavender perfume, quite apart from the suppression of unpleasant smells.

Sir William Temple, in his Essays on Health, recommended that the use of scent could well be applied to medical practise in quite a different way, as a cure for depression. He gave as example once visiting India House in Amsterdam amongst nutmegs, cloves and other spices and being completely refreshed in spirit by their aromatic scents.

Writing in 1656, William Coles said: 'Herbs do comfort the wearied brain with fragrant smells that yield a certain kind of nourishment'; and Lawson, in The Country Housewife, recommended dividing the garden into halves, one containing flowers suitable for nosegays and garlands, the other aromatic plants for distilling. He goes on to list twenty-six aromatic plants 'of good smell'.

6. OTHER HEALTH-GIVING PROPERTIES OF AROMATICS

Aromatics were put to many practical uses in the mediaeval household and later. Rosemary was popular: 'To preserve youth', wrote William Langham, whose *Garden of Health* appeared during Shakespeare's lifetime, 'make a box of the wood and smell it'. Rosemary seeds were placed in muslin bags and hung about a bedroom because they were thought to bring on sound sleep. And Thomas Newton, in *A Butler's Recipe Book*, suggested distilling the seed or the flowers, when the water 'drunk morning and evening, first and last, will make the breath very sweet'. It was also used to rub into the hair to promote its growth, and clothes and linen were washed in its water.

Above all, the peculiar property of reviving flagging spirits which aromatics possess was appreciated. A manuscript in the library of Trinity College, Cambridge, sent by the Countess of Hainault to her daughter, the wife of Edward III, describes the virtues of rosemary in numerous ways. Its scent was said to 'uplift the spirits', acting in the same way as smelling salts, and a sprig was always carried by the Queen.

Francis Bacon said that a garden of scented flowers and leaves 'is the greatest refreshment of the spirits of man', the scent of flowers and leaves acting in the same way as pleasant music.

Thomas Hyll in *The Profitable Art of Gardening* (1568) wrote that the greatest pleasure to be obtained from a garden was from the 'delight of walking in the same which both giveth health to man's body, and recovereth of strength after long sickness, by commodity of taking the fresh ayre and sweet smells' – and indeed, this is so. I have often been impressed by those who, for instance, suffered so terribly in the persecutions in Europe in the years before, and during the Second World War and who, when interviewed, replied that it was to a garden of scented flowers and leaves they had turned to above all else as a means of reviving their spirits and bringing comfort to their aching hearts.

Rosemary water is made by removing a handful of the tips of the new shoots in summer, placing in a saucepan one-third filled with water and simmering over a very low fire or flame. Cover with a lid to retain the fragrance and remove the pan after half an hour so that too much moisture does not evaporate. Allow to cool, then bottle and use as required.

In Hamlet, Ophelia says 'There's rosemary, that's for remembrance', and each year on April 23rd, St George's Day and also Shakespeare's birthday, the people of Stratford-on-Avon walk in procession through the town, wearing sprigs of rosemary and carrying posies of fragrant flowers and leaves, preceded by a band and the town beadle dressed in crimson livery. They make their way to the Church of the Holy Trinity where Shakespeare was baptised and where he is buried, and there place on his grave rosemary and the posies which they have carried around the town.

Both in France and in England at the time, it was customary to decorate the bodies of the dead with rosemary as it will remain fresh and fragrant longer than any other herb and because it was a herb of perpetual remembrance – hence the saying, 'keeping the memory green'.

PART TWO

The Aromatic Herb Garden

Richard Surfleet, in *The Country Farmer* (1599) describes the pleasure to be obtained by those who live in the country. 'It is a commendable and seemly thing to behold out of a window, many acres of ground well tilled and husbanded ... yet more fair to behold delightful borders of lavender, rosemary, box and such like ...'

A well laid out garden of aromatic herbs is indeed a delight; it is a particular joy to those who are partially sighted, or blind. It must be carefully planned for maximum effect and use.

1. LAYOUT OF THE GARDEN

The herb garden is usually made in one part of the garden as a special feature, possibly enclosed on two or more sides by a stone or brick wall or by panels of interwoven fencing to give protection from cold winds. The fence should be erected on the side from which the cold prevailing winds usually blow and arranged so that the plants are not deprived of sunlight. This is necessary to ripen the plants and to bring out the maximum amount of fragrance. Most herbs do better in dryer parts of the country than in the moister but warmer climates. Possibly the herb garden can be made so that it is reached through a rustic archway clothed with honeysuckle.

The total area of the herb garden need not be more than the size of a small sitting room, about 18 ft. × 12 ft. or 15 ft. square (Bacon wrote 'the herb garden is best square') with a central area of flagstones enclosed by borders of herbs 4 ft. wide. This will allow for an area of 49 sq. ft. to be covered by flagstones which will allow

ample space for a bird bath or some other distinctive
feature to be placed in the centre.

Paths and surfaces

There should be a short path leading from the entrance to
the paved area and this too can be covered with 2 ft. ×
2 ft. flagstones or with York stone. This should be laid
on a bed of sand with the stones set as close together as
possible to prevent the appearance of weeds, though a 2
in. × 2 in. hole should be left here and there in which to
plant aromatics of a carpeting habit.

Old bricks, placed on their side, will also make a distinctive path and here again holes should be left, allowing
2–3 ft. between each one, to take carpeting plants. It was
Francis Bacon, in his essay Of Gardens (1625), who
wrote of 'those plants which perfume the air most delight-
fully . . . being trodden upon and crushed, are burnet, wild
thyme and water mint . . .' and he suggested planting
alleys of them. By setting a number of plants in a path, the
maximum use of the ground will be obtained.

A brick or stone path is much superior to grass, for the
aromatic herbs are seen to advantage in all the glorious
hues of their foliage if they are allowed to grow over the
paths; this is not possible where grass is used to enclose
the beds. Again, once laid, a path of stone or brick will
need no further attention, whereas grass needs cutting
every few days in summer. Stone or brick paths allow the
herb garden to be enjoyed even in wet weather, though
this is not usually a suitable time to gather aromatics. If
making a stone or brick path, it will be easier if the
materials are of similar thickness for the surface must be
level for ease in walking.

First mark out the width of the path using garden lines; then, taking one section at a time, remove the soil to just below the depth of the stone (or bricks) and cover with an inch of builder's sand into which the stones are pressed after placing them with the sides in as straight a line as possible. It will be easier if the whole of the central area is to be covered with stone for there will not then be as many edges to keep straight.

Another way of making a path is to use shingle or gravel; this is inexpensive yet looks quite attractive. Remove the soil to a depth of 3 in. and spread the gravel to this depth. It will suppress weeds and enable the herbs to be tended during wet weather. The herbs may also be allowed to grow over the gravel path without harm.

Amongst the best plants for a path are the prostrate thymes, especially *Thymus serpyllus coccineus* with its mats of dark green and masses of tiny red flowers. Pink *Chintz*, too, is lovely and bears salmon-pink flowers. Also *T. doerfleri*, with its aromatic foliage of grey-green and flowers of pinkish-red. Set them about 3 ft. from each other, for they will soon spread out to cover an area of 2 ft. square or more.

The basil thyme, *Calamintha acinos*, is equally at home growing between stones, and enjoys dry conditions. A plant of almost prostrate habit, it bears purple flowers in whorls and when walked upon its foliage releases a refreshing menthol fragrance.

The Corsican savory, *Satureia rupestris*, an almost prostrate shrublet which bears tiny spikes of pure white in late summer, also releases a delicious minty scent when trodden upon. The Corsican mint, *Mentha requieni*, is equally aromatic but it likes moisture and a little decayed manure should be inserted around the roots at planting time. It forms mats of brilliant green, studded with tiny mauve flowers, and releases a powerful peppermint scent when trodden upon.

Chamomile may be used for a path as well as in the herb garden, where it is planted to give ground cover and to suppress weeds. For paving, the non-flowering dwarf chamomile, *Anthemis nobilis Treneague*, is the best form as it makes a spreading mat of emerald green and releases a refreshing apple perfume when walked upon. Indeed, in Spain, where it is common, it is called Manzinella, 'little apple', and before the introduction of tobacco its leaves were dried and smoked, the rich aroma was said to be a cure for sleeplessness.

A chamomile lawn

Chamomile was used in Tudor times to make an aromatic lawn, which Shakespeare said Falstaff was wont to walk upon and it is more than likely that Drake played his famous game of bowls upon a chamomile lawn, for grass lawns were rare in Tudor times. Indeed, the first grass lawns as we know them were not made until the reign of James I, the earliest description of the making of a lawn being given by Gervase Markham in 1613. Even during John Evelyn's lifetime, and he lived into the eighteenth century, paths and lawns were still made of chamomile. He wrote: 'it will now [October] be time to beat, roll and mow carpet walks of chamomile'.

To make a chamomile 'lawn', seed is sown in April, an ounce of seed producing about a thousand plants. First mark out the area of the 'walk' or 'lawn' required, then scatter the seed thinly. Rake in and keep moist and, where there is overcrowding, thin the plants to 6 in. apart, using the seedlings to move to those areas where the plants may be sparse. When the plants are established, roll them often and keep them free from weeds during the first year, at the end of which they will have spread out and will suppress all weeds from then onwards. When the plants are well established, clip them twice a year, which will encourage them to spread out and, in the second year, they may be walked or sat upon, which will make them release their fruity perfume.

Hedges and walls

Another attractive way of making a herb garden is to surround it (or one side of it) with a stone wall made about 3 ft. high. It should be built with a core filled with rubble and topped with 12 in. of soil as the wall is built; along the top aromatic herbs are planted. These may include the wall germanders, *Teucrium chamaedrys* with its glossy dark green foliage and *T. lithospermifolia*, which has silvery foliage and bears deep pink flowers.

T. chamaedrys was used in Tudor and Stuart times to make the dwarf hedges used in knot gardens, usually with hyssop or marjoram, for, as Thomas Hyll wrote in the *Art of Gardening*, 'these will endure all the winter through greene'. Parkinson, writing in 1629, said of the knotted germander beds of his time 'they must be kept in some form and proportion by cutting and the cuttings are much used as strewing herbs for houses, being pretty and sweet, with a refreshing lemony scent'. Wall germander was recommended by Sir Hugh Platt to grow in pots in rooms, whilst the leaves may be dried and used in pot-pourris, with those of balm, to which they impart a similar lemony scent. The early writers said that, like

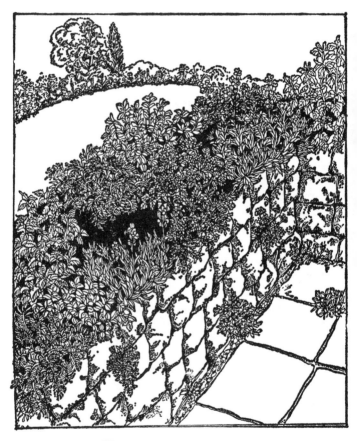

Wall Herb Garden

Eva Fliegen
The girl who lived on the scent of flowers

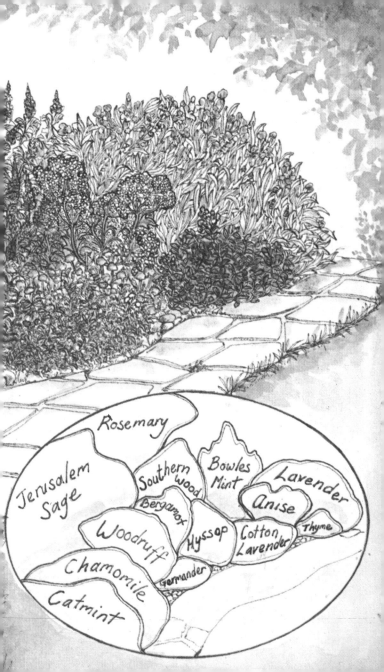

Rosemary

Jerusalem
Sage

Southern
wood

Bowles
Mint

Lavender

Bergamot

Anise

Woodruff

Hyssop

Cotton
Lavender

Thyme

Chamomile

Germander

Catmint

Lemon Verbena—*Lippia citriodora*
This aromatic shrub is one of the pleasantest and most popular
of scented plants. The leaves dry well to retain their inimitable
scent and flavour

rosemary, it was able to 'lift the spirits'; the dried leaves were used in sachets, to be carried in the pocket or hand-bag.

Germander makes a small bushy plant less than 10 in. tall; to keep it dwarf, clip it. This is done in April and again in July for the more often it is clipped the bushier it will become.

For a tall hedge, several of the taller growing lavenders which grow to 4 ft. in height may be planted, possibly to divide the aromatic garden from the rest of the garden. Lavender blends admirably with modern hybrid tea roses, especially those bearing fragrant red or pink flowers such as Wendy Cussons and Prima Ballerina, plants which have the same old world charm as the lavenders. My rose garden is bordered on all sides by a dense lavender hedge which protects the roses from strong winds with little or no damage to the lavender, which bears masses of deep purple spikes at the same time as the roses are in bloom.

Plant the robust Old English and Grappenhall varieties 3–4 ft. apart; they will join up within two years.

Lavender is of course invaluable in the garden. The stems may be burnt to scent a room (the tall Old English variety is most suitable for this). They are placed on lengths of old sheet or sacking and removed to a dry, airy room. Here they are left for several weeks to complete their drying, when the flowers are rubbed off and used to make up sachets to place amongst bedding and clothing. The stems should be kept to their full lengths and tied into bundles. If dried correctly, they will smoulder like sticks of incense.

The French marjoram *Origanum onites* may be grown on a wall and may also be used for a dwarf hedge. It is perennial, growing to 15 in. tall, but may be kept low by clipping. Slow to grow from seed, it is best propagated by root division or from cuttings rooted in sandy soil. It is also known as the pot marjoram and it has a pungent, minty scent to use in pot-pourris.

On a wall and also for a low hedge the cotton lavender *Santolina incana* with its rich grey foliage, like multitudes of tiny lamb's tails, can also be clipped into shape and is evergreen. The flowers, like bright yellow buttons and borne in large heads, are most handsome but have an unpleasant smell, like most of the Composites, which attracts flies for their pollination. In France it is called *garde-robe,* for its highly pungent foliage will keep away moths from clothes, whilst the sprigs will keep carpets free from moths, if placed around the sides. Tusser included it in his *Five Hundred Points of Good Husbandry* as being one of the best of the strewing herbs. The dried leaves are also used in pot-pourris and may be incorporated in a herb mixture for smoking, together with coltsfoot and chamomile. If placed in muslin bags to put amongst clothes, mix with it some lavender and rosemary flowers; it will give off a most agreeable perfume.

If used as a low hedge, plant 18 in. apart and clip into shape in April; or remove any long stems as they form, using secateurs to do so as the stems are tough and woody. The variety Weston is especially handsome, with its brilliant silver-grey foliage whilst Lemon Queen has lemon-yellow flowers. It is readily propagated from cuttings, removed with a 'heel' in July and rooted in sandy soil.

The dwarf lavenders may also be grown on a wall, especially *Lavendula nana alba,* the tiny white variety which makes a dainty rounded bush only 6 in. tall. It is the dwarf form of *L. alba.* Also suitable for a wall is Twickle Purple with its loose habit and stems of brilliant purple flowers, which are highly aromatic.

The dwarf artemesia *A. schmidtii nana* is also suitable for a wall, where its silver-grey foliage may be seen at its best, and it is deliciously pungent too. Likewise *Achillea Moonshine* with its densely silvered fern-like leaves.

Each of these wall plants may also be grown on the top of a high wall, perhaps in pockets formed by the weathering of the stone and also on a rock garden where their silvered foliage acts as a pleasing foil to the red and pink flowering plants.

One that should not be omitted for this purpose is the rock hyssop *H. aristatus*, which grows only 6–8 in. high, its deep blue flowers, contrasting with the dark foliage, much loved by the bees.

Aromatics to grow against walls and trellises

Against the walls of a herb garden or planted against trellis or inter-woven fencing, rosemary is at its loveliest. It will grow 6 ft. tall and the stems may be tied in as they grow; or plant it at both sides of an entrance so that, when passing, one's clothes may brush against it and release its delicious fragrance. When its foliage is dry, the plant will also release its scent when moved by the breezes. In olden times, it was allowed to grow against every sunny wall of house and garden. Paul Hentzner in his *Travels* (1598) wrote that at Hampton Court it was 'so planted and nailed to the walls as to cover them entirely' and being evergreen, it was colourful all the year round. It figures prominently in the manufacture of Eau de Cologne, favourite scent of the Emperor Napoleon Bonaparte, possibly because he was a native of Corsica, on which island rosemary abounds, growing amongst the rocks into dense bushes 6 ft. tall and the same in width.

He appreciated most of all, its cooling qualities and after washing would pour it over his neck and shoulders. A quarterly account for 1810 shows that Chardin his perfumer, supplied the Emperor with twelve dozen bottles of Eau de Cologne and later, a bill for supplying one hundred and eight cases, each of six bottles.

Eau de Cologne began as *Aqua 'Admirabilis* at the beginning of the eighteenth century when the brothers Johann Maria and Johann Baptiste Farina moved their business as makers of the famed elixir to Cologne from Santa Maria Maggiore in Italy. The elixir became popular during the Seven Years War when troops quartered in Cologne took away bottles of the Water to give to their families. It consists of otto of neroli mixed with ottos of rosemary and bergamot, dissolved in grape spirit. Bergamot was produced in Lombardy, from the rind of the bergamot orange. The green-tinted otto has a most refreshing smell, like that of rosemary with which it blends admirably.

Rosemary is believed to have taken its name from the Virgin Mary who is said to have rested against a bush and covered it with her cloak on the flight into Egypt though in reality it takes its name from *ros-marinus* 'dew of the sea' for it grows especially well in a salt-laden atmosphere and does well in a coastal garden.

It prefers a dry soil and one containing plenty of lime or lime rubble (mortar) which should be placed about its roots at planting time. Protection from cold wind is necessary or the foliage may be 'burnt' by north-easterly winds. Plant at least 3–4 ft. apart, preferably in spring. The flowers are like tiny purple-white orchids and appear early in summer in graceful spikes. There is a variety, Miss Jessop's Upright, which grows tall and spire-like, whilst *prostratus* grows almost flat on the ground – so plant it near a path.

Cuttings removed with a 'heel' will root in three months.

A good plant to grow against a trellis is wormwood, *Artemesia absinthium,* which stays handsome all winter with its 3 ft. stems clothed in grey-green leaves composed of many segments or lobes. The stems tend to be rather floppy and are best tied in as they grow. As a tonic, it was appreciated by all, wormwood 'tea' sweetened with honey being a popular drink of manor house and cottage; wormwood wine was made by steeping two pounds of leaves in two gallons of red wine for three to four months, then straining and using. The dried leaves placed amongst clothes and bedding would keep away moths and fleas, whilst a few sprigs hung up in a room would keep it free from flies all summer. Wormwood was described in John Josselyn's *New England's Rarities Discovered* (1672) and it became naturalised in America at an early date. It is used to make absinthe.

2. THE AROMATIC HERB BORDER

The border of an aromatic herb garden where there is no space problem should be its greatest adornment, both visually and for the purpose of growing the widest possible range of aromatics. Planning is, again, essential, for while the aromatics are good-tempered and will not mind being transplanted, it is better to establish them in their final place.

It is important to allow all herbs ample room to grow, so that all parts of the plants may receive the maximum of air and sunlight, and so that they do not grow into each other. If there is overcrowding, the plants soon begin to form patches of decay where they touch other plants, and will die back. Herb plants may be only small when they arrive from the grower; and so the inexperienced usually plant them too near together. Again, if they are allowed ample room, the full beauty of the plants, the interesting foliage shapes and equally varied colours can be seen to advantage. And always plant in early spring when the roots are active after their winter rest; the plants will grow away at once.

It is one of the virtues of most herbs that their soil requirements are quite simple – a well drained soil is essential but no fresh or artificial manure is needed. Indeed, aromatics in particular achieve their maximum of fragrance in a poor soil, provided it contains a little humus, which may be given as peat, used hops or old mushroom bed compost. This should be worked in as the ground is made ready in autumn, at the same time as all perennial weeds are removed. Then, each year in spring, give a light top dressing of any of these forms of humus.

Another important factor in growing herbs is that they are able to withstand long periods of drought and high summer temperatures. Once planted, they also require very little attention, and usually their harvesting will give them all the pruning necessary. The plants may be tidied up in spring when any further clipping is done. It is advisable to allow any long or untidy shoots to remain on the plants over winter, to give protection from frosts and cold winds.

Though a large number of aromatics are native of the warm Mediterranean regions and Near East, most of them are able to withstand an average winter in a moderate climate, though the plants are not tolerant of cold winds. These cause the foliage to 'brown' and may result in breakage of the stems of lavender and other plants with woody stems.

The back of the border

To the back, plant the taller growing herbs; wormwood, if it is not to be grown against a trellis and the bergamots, *Monarda didyma* and its lovely varieties, of which Cambridge Scarlet is the most striking. It was named in honour of Dr Nicholas Monardes of Seville who published his famous *Herbal on the Flora of America* in 1569; the name 'bergamot' is from the likeness of its fragrance to that of the bergamot orange used in the making of Eau de Cologne. The plant is a native of North America, where its leaves were used to make tea by those living about Lake Ontario. The Rev. William Hanbury wrote in 1769 that 'it should be propagated plentifully . . .

for the sake of the leaves, to make tea which is highly agreeable and refreshing'. Enjoy it cold, with a few drops of lemon juice and neither milk nor sugar.

The bergamot grows 3 ft. tall and requires a soil containing more humus than other herbs, to retain summer moisture.

Tansy and costmary are others for the back of a border and possess a charm of their own, though they are now rarely found in our gardens. Tansy (*Tanacitum vulgare*) is a much-branched perennial growing 3 ft. tall with dark green fern-like leaves which release a powerful aromatic smell when handled. The scent is camphor-like and is released from glandular dots when the leaves are pressed. It takes its name from the Greek *athanasia*, immortal, because it remains so long in bloom. Tusser included it amongst his 'herbs for strewing' as the leaves drive away insects and will release their camphor smell when trodden upon. They have another use today; when soaked in buttermilk for ten days, they make an excellent and soothing complexion milk or 'after-shave'. Coles, in his *Art of Simpling* rightly said that it would make 'the complexion very fair'.

Costmary grows to a similar height and has entire leaves of deep green. It bears flat heads of deep yellow flowers. Native of Central Asia, it has been a garden plant possibly since Roman times. Dedicated to St Mary Magdalene, it has had many botanical names; the most common in current use is *Chrysanthemum balsamita*. Like the closely related tansy, it was used to impart its balsamic flavour to ale; hence another name, alecost.

In the *Paradisus*, Parkinson describes the delightful custom of tying together small bundles of costmary, lavender and rosemary 'to lie upon the tops of beds'; I think he meant on pillows, there to impart their fragrance. The bundles were also placed amongst clothing and bedding to impart a rich, aromatic perfume.

Near costmary, plant mugwort which also grows 3–4 ft. tall, its dark green pinnate leaves covered in silvery down on the underside. Like alecost, it was once used to clarify ale before hops came to do this better; a nourishing beer can be made from it, of the dried leaves to two gallons of water. Simmer for an hour, add one pound of brown sugar and strain into an earthenware container. Add a tablespoon of yeast and allow to ferment for ten days, then strain into bottles, cork, and keep for a month before using.

The plant takes its name from the Saxon 'moughte', a moth, for, as Dioscorides said, 'it does keep moths from clothes' and a sprig placed in a button-hole each morning will keep away flies for the whole day. It was one of the nine sacred herbs and was hung up to protect the house from evil.

Jerusalem sage, *Phlomis fruticosa,* is a tall stately plant of shrub-like habit, often reaching 5 ft. in height, forming a dense bush with grey-green aromatic foliage, and bearing in dense whorls double-lipped yellow flowers visited by the bees. The sage-like leaves are covered with rusty down. It requires a light soil, when it should be fully perennial. Its leaves are used in pot-pourris and have an incense-like pungency.

The taller lavenders recommended for a hedge are also suitable for the back of the herb border. Allow at least 3–4 ft. between the plants.

Near the grey-leaved lavenders plant the rue, *Ruta graveolens,* for I know of no other garden plant that has foliage of richer blue. A well grown plant will reach 2–3 ft. in height and makes a rounded bush, handsome with its divided leaves which release an intense bitterness when pressed. Because of this, rue was known as the herb of repentance, or herb of grace. Due to its antiseptic qualities, sprigs of rue were placed in the dock at Assize Court during an outbreak of gaol fever at Newgate Prison in 1750.

The form Jackman's Blue is even of deeper metallic blue and grows 2 ft. tall; this is not quite as tall as the lovely variegated form, the leaves taking on contrasting shades of cream and yellow.

The sages grow to a similar height and should be planted at the front of the back row herbs. Walfred Strabo wrote from his monastery on the shore of Lake Constance, in the ninth century, 'amongst my herbs, sage holds place of honour; of good scent it is and full of virtue for many ills'. *Salvia officinalis* it is botanically, from the Latin for salvation, for the plant was thought to give long life to all who used it.

Sage cordial, made by boiling half a pound of fresh leaves with honey and a little lemon juice, may be taken warm to ease a tight chest and will help to cure a cold; if used as a gargle, it will ease a sore throat. If taken cold, a wineglassful acts as a refreshing tonic drink, delicious in summer if ice is added.

Sage leaves may be used in pot-pourris; *S. rutilans*, the pineapple sage, is especially recommended, for the leaves really do have the powerful scent of ripe pineapples. The plant grows 2 ft. tall but unfortunately is not as hardy as the other sages.

The best of all the sages is *S. officinalis purpurea* which has purple-red stems and sage-green leaves shot with crimson. There is a golden form, *aurea*, and an attractive variegated form with leaves of carmine, cream and green. They grow 2 ft. tall and have blue flower spikes in summer. All are most decorative.

The sages are propagated from cuttings and from seed. Plant 2 ft. apart, and, as they require a light well drained soil for a long life, give a mulch each year, as sages are shallow rooting.

Aromatics of middle height

An enchanting middle row plant is southernwood or Lad's Love, *Artemisia abrotanum*, with its finely divided foliage, like filigree silk and of a lovely soft green colour. Strabo said 'it has well-nigh as many virtues as leaves' not least of which is its ability to bring about sound sleep if the fresh (or dried) leaves are placed in a muslin bag beneath the pillow case; they may also be placed amongst clothing to keep away moths; in this respect it acts as efficiently as cotton lavender. Southernwood gives its pungent lemony scent to pot-pourris and, if simmered in water together with some rosemary and massaged into the scalp, it will do more than anything to prevent hair falling out.

Try this old idea for perfuming a room. It is too lovely a plant to be cut heavily, but occasionally it may be necessary to shorten an unduly long or broken shoot (this is best done in winter or spring when the leaves will have fallen). First dry the stems before cutting into small pieces 2–3 in. long which, if placed on a low fire (embers are better), will release its refreshing scent about a room which is more appreciated at the end of a tiring day.

No plant has a more delicious smell when the leaves are pressed, but unfortunately it loses its leaves in winter. They reappear in May when the woody stems may be removed and trimmed to 6 in. long for inserting in sandy compost; they will root in two months.

Not quite so tall growing is *Artemesia borealis*, which has even more finely divided foliage of a deeper grey-green colouring, though it has not so pronounced a perfume. For all that, it is a most handsome plant for the border, likewise Lady's Maid which also grows about 20 in. tall.

Hyssop should be in every border for its short racemes of clearest blue (and pink) are much visited by bees and butterflies. An evergreen, growing 20 in. tall, it is native of the cooler parts of Central Europe. It was mentioned so often in the Bible that it took its name from the Hebrew, *azob*, a holy plant.

Michael Drayton, wrote 'hyssop is a herb most prime' for all parts are scented. The dried flowers and the leaves are used in pot-pourris, for they have a pleasant pungent smell; they were much in demand for strewing over the floor of church pew and manor house.

Hyssop is propagated from cuttings and by seed, sown (like sage) in shallow drills in April and transplanted 2 ft. apart, for the plants grow quite bushy. Plant it near the curry plant, *Helichrysum angustifolium*, an almost hardy perennial with attractive grey foliage and bearing small yellow everlasting flowers in mid-summer. Use the leaves in pot-pourris.

White horehound, *Marrubium vulgare*, is equally attractive with its oval, bluntly-toothed leaves and square stems covered in woolly down, which gives the plant a frosted appearance. The tiny white flowers, borne in dense whorls, are much visited by bees.

When warmed by the sun, the leaves emit a musky fragrance and from them a tonic beer is brewed. Equally invigorating is horehound tea; to make it, gather one ounce of fresh leaves and pour over them a pint of boiling water. Add a little lemon juice, strain and drink either hot

or cold which, in summer, is most refreshing if a few
pieces of ice are added.

Aromatics of compact habit

For the front of the border, plant the marjorams anywhere, for they have so many uses and attract bees and
butterflies. The sweet or 'knotted' marjoram, *Origanum
majorana*, has an aromatic scent that is particularly refreshing in warm weather; it secretes an essential oil from
the stems and leaves that forms a deposit of crystalline
matter, stearoptane, with a smell of camphor. Gerard described the plant as 'marvellous sweet' and Parkinson
said that it was much in demand with the ladies 'to put in
nosegays' and to use in sweet powders, sweet bags and
sweet washing waters. It was in fact, the great standby for
the making of most toilet requisites. It was also known as
the 'knotted' marjoram, not because it was used to make
the knot garden of the Tudors but because the tiny brown
buds of the flowers when first appearing on the stems are
like knots of string.

Philippe Gutbert, the Physician Regent in Paris early in
the seventeenth century, has given us an excellent pre-
scription for making a scented talcum powder using marjoram. It is 'take 2 lbs. of orris root, ground to a powder; 2
ozs. of (dried) sweet marjoram; 2 ozs. calamus root; ½ lb.
of scented rose petals which have been dried; ½ dram of
cloves and of musk'. Pound together until the whole has
become a sweet scented powder which will retain its perfume for a year or more.

The native marjoram, *O. vulgare*, is taller growing and
is occasionally found on downlands, appearing quite red-
dish from a distance. Its botanical name means 'joy of the

mountains' and, wherever it is found, it is a joy to behold and so refreshing to smell when one is tired on a warm day. A handful of leaves in a warm bath will bring contentment to tired limbs and an infusion of the leaves in boiling water will, if a wineglassful is taken at bedtime, bring about sound sleep.

The pot marjoram, *O. onites*, is more vigorous still, growing about 18 in. tall; its leaves are more pungent than sweet. There is a striking golden form which lends a splash of brilliant colour to the aromatic garden in spring and early summer; it loses its golden hue in winter.

The marjorams may be grown from seed sown in shallow drills in April, or from cuttings, or by root division in spring.

With mint and rosemary, sweet marjoram was one of the most popular scents for vinaigrettes. Of French origin, they became popular in England during Regency times, for carrying in the pocket to hold to the nose should it be necessary 'to correct the bad quality of air' or to refresh one's head if suffering from a cold or where the air was oppressive. Later, the vinaigrette gave way to the smelling bottle of today. The vinaigrettes held a sponge soaked in aromatic vinegar made by distilling acetate of copper. This was aromatised with otto of lavender, rosemary, mint or marjoram after first dissolving a small amount of camphor in the vinegar (acetic acid).

A home-made smelling bottle may be made by taking a handful of fresh leaves of any of these plants and immersing them in rectified spirit (obtainable from a chemist) for about ten days. Then add a little acetic acid and, after four to five days, strain and use a little on a piece of sponge placed in a small bottle. The idea was popular at a much earlier date for George Cavendish, faithful attendant of Cardinal Wolsey, has told us that his master always carried about with him a sponge filled with scented vinegar.

The Elizabethans kept their scented waters in small bottles of chastened silver, one of the finest examples of which, dating from about 1565, is to be seen in the Victoria and Albert museum in London.

The pot marigold, *Calendula officinalis,* an annual, is a colourful plant with its pale green leaves and orange or yellow flowers with their rayed petals. All parts are pungent and at one time the dried flowers were sold from barrels at a penny an ounce, in every grocer's and apothecary's shop. Marigold water made from fresh flowers is soothing (used lukewarm) to tired eyes, and marigold tea at bedtime promotes sound sleep. Marigold essence in soaps and hand creams is soothing and healing and softens the skin.

The plant is so hardy that it will stand over winter and continue flowering whenever the sun shines upon it. It will also sow itself, and usually behaves as a biennial.

Tusser said it should be grown in pots and kept on the kitchen sill all the year round.

Another annual which must be included among the aromatics is coriander, *Coriandrum sativum,* which grows 9–10 in. tall, with branched stems and cut leaves. At one time it was grown commercially for its scented seeds which were put in childrens' sweets. Only the seed (when dry) is aromatic, the rest of the plant being unpleasant smelling. The seeds are still used for flavouring, and were one of the ingredients of Carmelite Water. George Wilson, apothecary to James II, made a celebrated Honey Water which, in his words 'made soft the skin and gives one of the most agreeable scents that can be smelt'. He made it by dissolving honey in warm water, straining and adding essence of musk, a few cloves, a few drops of vanilla, coriander seeds (after keeping them for six months), orange-water and a little alcohol. It makes a soothing after-shave lotion and carries a refreshing masculine perfume.

An old recipe to make scented bags to place amongst linen and clothes was to take '2 ounces of coriander seed; 2 of orris root; 2 of scented rose leaves; 2 of calamus; together with a drachm of mace, cinnamon and musk; a drachm of white sugar; and half an ounce of lavender flowers and the same of dried rose root (*Sedum rhodiola*). Pound well together and place the powder in small muslin bags.'

In the British Museum there is an old coriander recipe for a powder which was used by Queen Isabella of Spain in the sixteenth century: 'Take 4 ounces of (dried) scented rose leaves; half an ounce of orris root, calamus, clove-scented pinks, storax and coriander and pound and mix together.' The result is a sweet scented powder which, in sachets or bags, will long retain its perfume.

Coriander is raised by sowing seeds in April where the plants are to mature. Sow a few seeds in a circle of 15 in. diameter and thin to 4 in. apart around the circumference.

Another annual is anise, *Pimpinella anisum*, which grows 15 in. tall, with finely serrated leaves and white flowers which open star-like. The fruit is small with a peculiar aromatic scent due to the presence of anisic aldehyde. The dried seeds (aniseed balls) coated with sugar have been a favourite children's sweet since early times. The seeds have long been used to flavour liqueurs.

Native of the Near East, it was mentioned in St Matthew and was widely grown for its ability to destroy lice amongst bedding and about one's clothes.

Aniseed 'tea' is made by pouring boiling water on to a

teaspoonful of seed. Taken when hot, it will ease a tight chest, and when cold, it is excellent for digestive disorders.

Seed is sown in April and the plants thinned to 10 in. apart. The seed ripens only in a dry sunny climate like that of South East of England, but not wetter parts.

The catmints will give an air of softness to any border with their grey-green foliage and loose, informal habit. When the short purple-blue flower spikes appear early in summer, the plants take on a delightful misty appearance.

The native *Nepeta cataria*, called the catmint because cats love to roll about the foliage in summer and enjoy eating the leaves, grows 18 in. tall and is strongly aromatic, its leaves having a pungent smell, lightened with a refreshing lemony scent. A delicious tonic 'tea' is made by pouring a pint of boiling water on to the leaves and drinking it either hot or cold. It is a refreshing drink when ice cold in summer. When hot, 'catnip tea' was the countryman's remedy for a cold.

N. mussinii grows only 10–12 in. tall and is a better border plant. The leaves retain their lemony scent when dry and may be used, with those of balm and marjoram, in pot-pourris and sweet bags. Balm, *Melissa officinalis*, grows about 18 in. tall, its deeply wrinkled leaves being palest green and deliciously lemon-scented. With alecost, it grew in every tavern garden, for its leaves were used to impart their aromatic scent to ale. It was also in constant use for strewing, for it releases its scent when walked upon whilst the juice from the stems was rubbed over oak furniture to impart a gloss and leave behind its refreshing perfume.

Evelyn wrote that it is 'sovereign for the brain, strengthening the memory and chasing away melancholy'.

Balm 'tea' acts as a splendid tonic and a wineglass at night settles the digestion and promotes sleep. Balm was used to make Hungary Water and Carmelite Water and the leaves, together with those of lemon thyme, rosemary and bay, and those of the lemon scented pelargoniums, may be used to make a delicious 'green' pot-pourri.

Balm makes a bushy plant and does better in a soil containing some humus for it needs moisture about its roots. It is propagated by division in spring.

The thymes are in every way delightful plants and Parkinson wrote, 'there is no herb of more use in the houses of high and low ... for bathing and for strewing'. Thymol, contained in the essential oil, ranks high as an antiseptic. A few drops of oil of thyme in a pint of boiling water will, if inhaled, bring instant relief to a blocked nose.

The tallest of the thymes grow only 9 in. high and amongst them *Thymus vulgaris* with its dark green leaves is best known. But it is *T. citriodorus* the lemon thyme, which is so often included in pot-pourris. There is a form *aureus,* with golden edged leaves, whilst Silver Queen is edged with white; both are lemon-scented. There are others, equally interesting. *T. erectus* has camphor-scented foliage and *T. fragrantissima* has leaves which are scented with orange. The less common *T. odoratissimus* has a delicious fruity perfume, whilst *T. herba barona* is caraway-scented. The thymes should be planted to the front of the border as they grow less than 6 in. tall; they are right for planting in a wheel herb garden or in window boxes. They are propagated from cuttings.

Woodruff, *Asperula odorata,* I love. It is a slender little plant; it appears so delicate and yet it is a perennial of considerable toughness. It grows only 6 in. tall, bearing its leaves on seemingly fragile stems in neat whorls, with

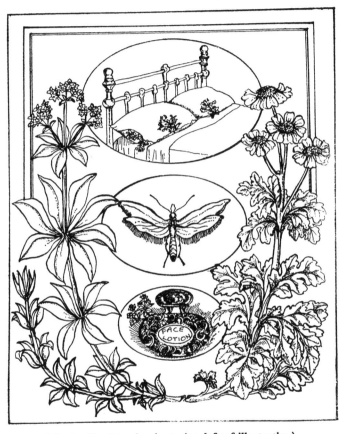

Woodruff – *Asperula odorata* (on left of illustration)
The whole herb dried has a scent of new-mown hay, due to
Coumarin. Bunches may be put amongst linen to impart a
pleasant scent. Feverfew – *Chrysanthemum parthenium* (on right
of illustration) The herb has golden-green foliage, white daisy
flowers and a pungent fresh smell.

tiny white flowers like fairy stars. It has the interesting
scent of newly mown hay which increases as the leaves
dry, due to the presence of coumarin. In fact, the longer
the leaves are kept the more intense does the fragrance
become, so that in sachets of dried leaves, together with
those of rosemary and lemon thyme, the mixture retains
its scent for years and may be placed between bed linen
and clothes or under a cushion. Tusser knew it as 'sweet
grass' and advised making a sweet water from the leaves
for bathing the face to improve the complexion. Johnston,
who revised and updated Gerard's *Herbal*, advised using
the leaves to sweeten clothes and bedding; and it can be
used as a moth deterrent. The leaves were also stuffed
into pillows, cushions and into mattresses.

Woodruff leaves were placed between book pages to relieve them of any mustiness if the books were kept in a
damp room.

Dr Fernie, the celebrated herbalist, said that the leaves
should be removed by cutting through the stems immedi-
ately above and below the whorl and this would retain
their star-like arrangement. A nice idea.

Woodruff is readily raised from seed sown in spring,
the plants being thinned to 4–5 in. apart. It is tolerant of
shade and may be grown with the mints. Of these, there
are many and each so interesting and different in their
scents. Some are suitable only for culinary use, such as the
apple mint and spearmint, whilst there are others which
are admirable for pot-pourris. Of these, perhaps the best
is Eau de Cologne or bergamot mint; its perfume is due to
the presence of citral as in lemon thyme and balm. Placed
in a bath, a few sprigs will release a scent of Eau de
Cologne and together with rosemary, the leaves may be
infused in hot water and used as a hair rinse, keeping the
scalp free from dandruff.

Peppermint is most probably a natural hybrid of *Mentha spicata*, the spearmint and *M. aquatica*, the water mint, and is present in East Anglia and the East Midlands of England. It was discovered as recently as 1700 and given its name by John Rea in his *History of Plants* (1704). The oil, which is used in peppermint sweets, also to relieve indigestion and to allay the feeling of sickness, was said by Dr Braddon to be 'the best, safest, and most agreeable of all antiseptics'. Menthol cones were at one time burnt in sick rooms, especially where there was difficulty with respiration.

The mints require a moist humus laden soil and grow best in partial shade, contrary to the conditions needed by most other herbs.

The savorys are aromatics of considerable interest, the winter savory with its sharp minty scent being used for strewing and to include in pot-pourris. This savory is perennial and quite hardy. It grows 9–10 in. tall with spreading branches, and in late summer bears purple-pink flowers in short racemes. The leaves, rubbed on wasp stings, give instant relief and an infusion of the leaves helps to ease the flow of urine where there is difficulty. Michael Drayton coupled the herb with tansy for they were generally used together in pot pourris and mixed with bread crumbs to cover meat when roasting, 'be it fish or flesh, to give it a quicker relish'.

Sweet waters were made from the fresh leaves which were also used in salads to which they lent interest and so useful was the plant that it was included in John Josselyn's list of these plants introduced into America by the early settlers.

Summer Savory is an annual requiring half hardy treatment for it is more tender than the winter variety. Although its leaves are pungent and may be used when dry in pot pourris, it is to impart their flavour to broad beans when cooking that the leaves are mostly used.

Featherfew is another pretty front of the border plant, growing 12–15 in. tall with pale green leaves and bearing its button-like flowers in terminal clusters. The plant was used in Gervase Markham's celebrated skin lotion, the first commercial beauty preparation. The dried leaves placed amongst clothes will keep away moths, whilst the distilled water made from the leaves was said to remove freckles and skin blemishes.

It is perennial, but is readily raised from seed sown in heat in February and planted out in early summer. During Victorian times, it was grown in this way for summer bedding.

There are many other delightful plants which are given the classification of herbs, plants such as fennel, parsley, tarragon and chives, but as they are grown entirely for their culinary and medicinal uses they do not concern us here.

Town gardens

Aromatic herbs may be grown with success in a town garden, provided it receives an average amount of sunlight. Like most vegetables, such herbs must be planted in the open, away from overhanging trees and the shade of nearby buildings.

One of the most attractive town gardens I know is comprised of a small courtyard covered with flagstones; at irregular intervals are placed oak tubs filled with aromatic plants and herbs of every description. It is a complete herb garden in every way and the plants are in constant use throughout the year. In addition, they enhance what otherwise would be an uninteresting yard at the rear of a small terrace house with the beauty of their foliage: the steel-blue of rue, the grey-green of wormwood, the silvered foliage of cotton lavender, the variegated leaf of the balm with its splashes of yellow and gold, all of them colourful and many of them retaining their foliage through the winter.

Growing in tubs

The area must have its fair share of sunlight – herbs never do well in shade, with but one or two exceptions – so place the tubs on the sunny side of the area. There are few aromatics which cannot be grown in tubs; only the most vigorous need be excluded and even these can be kept reasonably compact by clipping them in spring, though usually removing the stems when required will be all the pruning that is necessary.

The scented-leaf geraniums may be planted with the other aromatics and, if gardening in the warmer parts, they will come to no harm if left in the tubs all winter.

When planting the tubs, try to arrange the herbs so that in each tub there are plants of contrasting foliage colours. If a rosemary is planted in one tub, and it should be at the centre, then plant around the side of the tub *Santolina incana Weston*, the most compact of the cotton lavenders, or several plants of *Nepeta mussinii* which, with its grey foliage and misty blue flowers, is delightful when used in this way.

A wonderful effect is obtained by planting rue, Jackman's Blue, at the centre and surrounding it with sweet marjoram and its golden variety, *aureum*. Visitors to the 'garden' will make straight for this striking combination of foliage colours.

The sages could occupy one tub. At the centre plant *Salvia grahami* with its cheerful scarlet flowers and surround it with the 'red' variety, *purpurea*; with its plum coloured stems and leaves. Then around it set the gold-leaf sage which is so attractive with its lemon-coloured leaves.

The coloured-leaf thymes, planted 4–5 in. apart around the side are interesting in their many hues, especially *T. citriodorus aureus* and Silver Queen; both are deliciously lemon-scented.

Do not use too many plants in each tub, for most of them will quickly grow bushy and to plant too closely will make them deprive each other of sunlight.

Four or five tubs will ensure that there will be a suitable selection of plants to make up pot-pourris and sachets to place amongst linen and clothing. These may be made and given as gifts for birthdays and will be a most appreciated and lasting present so that you will continually be in the thoughts of the receiver. Another attractive present will be to raise aromatics from seed or cuttings and to grow them in small pots when five or six, each of them different, will make a greatly appreciated gift.

Oak tubs should be treated with Cuprinol, creosote or some other wood preservative. The tubs must be treated both on the inside and outside and the iron hoops with a rust-preventing paint before giving the hoops a coating of black paint. As tubs are usually of oak, they are better left in their natural state apart from treating them with preservative. To give them long life and to prevent water collecting about the base, place them on bricks, using three to each tub so that they will be quite secure and will not rock. Ensure, too, that they are drilled with several holes through which excess rain can escape, for herbs never do well in wet soil.

Before filling the tubs, place some broken crocks or bricks over the drainage holes to prevent them becoming choked with soil. Then fill the tubs with fibrous loam, or with specially prepared compost. If you are making up your own compost, mix in a little decayed manure, or old mushroom bed, compost or used hops from a brewery. Work in also some lime rubble (mortar), usually obtainable from old stone buildings which have been pulled down. If this is not obtainable, mix in some hydrated lime or crushed limestone, about one pound to each tub. Aromatics are great lime lovers and will not grow well in an acid soil. The soil of most town gardens will be of a high acid content, due to deposits of soot and sulphur over many years so, if possible, use fresh soil to fill the tubs.

If filled to within 2 in. of the top, this will allow for watering during dry weather without the soil splashing over the side. But it should be said that of all plants, the aromatics are better able to flourish in long periods of drought and, if the soil contains some humus, there will be little need for artificial watering. This enables one to be away from home for several weeks at a time without the plants coming to any harm. Only when the soil becomes really dry will there be a need to water; this is best done in late evening. Give the soil a thorough soaking. The plants will, however, benefit from a topping up of the compost in alternate years with a mixture of fibrous loam, decayed manure and some lime rubble to keep it sweet. This will act as a mulch.

The plants will also appreciate a gentle syringing when the weather is warm, again preferably in late evening; a simple way to protect the less hardy plants from frost and cold winds in winter is to cover them with large sheets of polythene, punctured with holes to release excess condensation. The sheets are tied to the tubs with strong twine and are removed when the weather becomes milder.

Window boxes

Where space is even more limited, window boxes may be used to grow the more compact aromatics, fixing them either inside or outside a sunny window; the boxes may also be placed on a verandah or terrace, or fixed to the sunny wall of a courtyard. With a window box, the herbs can be tended from the open window of a room or from outside if the window is low down. More colour will be enjoyed if one or two dwarf geraniums are grown with the aromatics. Most effective is the old Golden Harry Hieover, its golden leaves being zoned with bronze whilst, above, its scarlet flowers hover like tiny butterflies.

For window boxes, plant only the most compact of the aromatics, the thymes, marjoram and winter savory, *Santolina incana Weston*, the rock hyssop, *H. aristatus*, the tiny dwarf white lavender and the dwarf golden sage. If the variegated leaf varieties are also used, the selection will be quite large and will be most colourful throughout the year, for all these plants are evergreen.

A window box can be fixed to a wall outside the kitchen door where the plants may easily be tended. Fix the boxes by means of strong iron brackets. The boxes are made of strong wood, the size of the window or any reasonable size. Along the front and at the sides, pieces cut from logs with the bark attached, may be fixed to the boxes, to give a more pleasing appearance and to do away with the need to paint the box.

Similar boxes may be fixed to a sunny courtyard wall. Space the boxes so that the plants receive as much sunlight as possible. As long ago as 1594 Sir Hugh Platt wrote: 'in every window you may make square frames ... of boards, well pitched within. Fill with some rich earth and plant such flowers or herbs therein as you like best.' Window boxes made of lead and with a pleasantly worked front are now eagerly sought by collectors of garden antiques. But a window box of wood presents few difficulties.

The box should be constructed of 1 in. timber as it will have to carry a considerable weight of compost when filled. The wood will be cut to the required lengths, the two ends so that they will fit inside the back and front lengths. Remember that a good simple job is better than a bad complicated one and if any attempt is made to dovetail the corners, the strength of a dovetail lies in its construction and a water-resistant glue must be used. When securing the ends, there will be no advantage in using screws instead of nails for screws tend to split the wood. For additional strength at the corners, use an angle bracket, preferably inside.

Always use hardwood, seasoned oak or American Red Cedar, for boxes; these are impervious to moisture. Several drainage holes of $\frac{1}{2}$ in. diameter should be drilled in the base and crocks placed over them. Fix the box to the wall or window frame so that it will be quite secure when filled with soil. Use fresh fibrous loam to fill the box to almost the top and, for a box 3 ft. long and 6 in. deep, which are the minimum requirements, mix into the compost four ounces of bone meal or steamed bone flour and about one pound of ground limestone. April is a suitable time to make up and plant the boxes. The plants can be kept dwarf and tidy by regularly pinching out the shoots when required.

Large earthenware pots may also be used to grow aromatics; place them about an enclosed courtyard where they will not be blown over by wind. Terra cotta urns are especially attractive but are now difficult to find and at a reasonable price. There are also containers made of fibre glass and to ancient designs which are admirable when filled with aromatics and geraniums.

Hanging baskets and pots

Aromatics may also be grown in hanging baskets, suspended from the eaves of a house or from a wall so that

A Pleasant Setting for an Aromatic Hanging Basket

they are just above the height of a tall man. They are watered, and this will only occasionally be necessary, from a step-ladder. A basket of herbs may also be suspended from the ceiling above the kitchen sink and is a most attractive way of decorating a room with living plants. Wherever it is to be placed, the basket will need to be suspended by means of a strong hook.

The basket should be 18–20 in. diameter and made of strong galvanised wire. First line the basket with a thick layer of sphagnum moss which will absorb and retain moisture, then fill the basket almost to the top with fibrous loam to which a little peat has been mixed and a handful of mortar. Add a few pieces of charcoal to keep the soil sweet. Allow it several days to settle down before planting. The basket can more easily be prepared by standing it on top of a plant pot.

At the centre, place lemon balm and around it, hyssop, marjoram and thyme. If the basket is indoors, include sweet basil and around the sides plant alehoof, *Nepeta glechoma*, better known as ground ivy. It is a trailing plant which in the wild pulls itself along the ground, rooting at the leaf joints. From a basket it will trail down to several feet, and it is quite delightful with its grey-green aromatic leaves which, today, we use in pot-pourris.

Aromatics in pots may also be suspended from walls by brackets as the Elizabethans used to do. The custom was to fasten pots of rosemary, which grows well indoors, to the chimney on either side of a fireplace in summertime. It would keep the room cool and fragrant. We may have it indoors today, growing in pots in a jardiniere, to beautify a dull corner.

An idea for a small garden

The dwarf growing aromatics may be used in many attractive ways. One is to plant them in a circle of about 6 ft. in diameter, with rows from the centre to the circumference, radiating like the spokes of a cartwheel; discarded cartwheels were in fact used to make small herb garden when wooden wheels motivated every farm cart and they cost little to replace. Hyssop, cotton lavender, germander and French marjoram may all be used for the spokes and outer rim. A delightful idea is to alternate the spokes with green and golden (*aureum*) marjoram and to use one of the other aromatics for the circumference. In the spaces, other dwarf aromatics are planted. There will be eight spaces to fill. In one plant the golden thyme, *Thymus vulgaris aureum*, and in the next Silver Posie, with its silver variegated foliage and pink stems. Then French marjoram, if not used for the spokes; Santolina, Weston; rock hyssop; dwarf lavender; wall germander; the golden lemon-scented thyme, *T. citriodora aureus*, all being of neat, compact habit. The effect will be delightful and the plants long lasting and useful in so many ways.

A herb wheel could be made a centre piece of a lawn or any place where the sun shines down upon it.

4. LESS HARDY AROMATICS

There are a number of aromatics which are not entirely hardy in cooler climates such as that of the British Isles; these require, in winter, the protection of a greenhouse or living room, but they are well worth growing in spite of their tenderness. The most important of these plants are the delightful scented-leaf pelargoniums or geraniums; fresh or dried, the leaves release a delicious perfume. With scented-leaf pelargoniums, plant lemon verbena and bay, plants which are also not quite hardy, and rosemary, balm, lavender and southernwood.

Mrs Earle, whose charming and instructive books about her Surrey garden early this century endeared her to garden lovers everywhere, also left to us a recipe for a pot-pourri using scented-leaf geraniums. It is to take equal parts of table salt and borax powder (one ounce of each) and an eighth of an ounce of powdered cinnamon and mix well together. Then to each basinful of dried rose petals from the most fragrant varieties, scatter over them a dessertspoonful of the mixture and mix in a handful of the leaves of lemon scented verbena, lavender, thyme, rosemary and marjoram, scattering about them more of the powder until all is used up and there will be sufficient pot-pourri to fill a large jar or bowl. It will retain its fragrance for fully a year but should be turned daily for the scent to be truly appreciated.

The scented pelargoniums

The scented-leaf geraniums, which possess such a wide variety of perfumes and are so highly ornamental, deserve to be better known. They are not new plants; they have been grown in the windows of West Country cottages in England since they were first brought from Africa and the Mediterranean regions during the time of Charles I. They were then used for sweetening the damp, musty rooms of old cottages and manor houses, which for so long had relied on the bowls of delicious pot-pourri to provide indoor sweetness, especially during winter when there were few scented flowers in the garden. Today, in place of pot-pourri, still used in many of our great houses, we are given synthetic perfumed sprays to keep our homes sweet, but how much lovelier it would be to perfume rooms with living plants which the cottagers of the seventeenth century soon came to appreciate. The same delightful plants may be obtained today for a small price, robust and ready potted; and, if tended with care and given a frost-proof room, which almost all our living rooms are, the same plants should last almost a lifetime.

Quite happy in partial shade, the scented geraniums were particularly suited to the low ceilings of cottages with their thick walls and tiny windows which admit only the minimum of light. It is the leaves of the plant which are fragrant, not the flowers, which are quite insignificant; this means that there are few petals to fall and untidy the room. In fact, the only attention the plants require is occasional watering and even then geraniums should not be given water unless they really need it. Especially throughout winter the soil should be kept almost dry. At the beginning of June, when the fear of frost is over, the plants will appreciate repotting, and should be allowed to stand outdoors in a sheltered position for a full month or possibly more whilst the brilliant summer-flowered pelargoniums are being enjoyed indoors. Then, at the end of August, the plants may be taken indoors and will continue to add their fragrance to the rooms until the following June. The scented geraniums are ideal plants for the town flat or the home with a restricted garden, as they can remain indoors permanently, or may be permitted to enjoy the summer sunshine and rains by being placed on a verandah or in a small courtyard. They can also be grown in the open in exactly the same way as are the Paul Crampel and Gustav Emich geraniums, used so much for summer bedding, but being taller growing they should be given a sheltered situation. Whether to be grown on in the house or in a greenhouse, the plants must be lifted and potted before the frosts arrive.

When potting the plants, use if possible, a small quantity of well decayed manure, which sounds quite out of place when describing these fragrant plants, but they really do appreciate this. Or failing this, add some peat to the soil which should be a fibrous loam. The pots too must be well drained by placing broken crocks at the bottom. It is advisable to re-pot at the end of every winter, staking the plants if necessary, for several varieties grow tall, and cutting back any side shoots that may have grown too long so as to keep the plant in shape.

The Victorians, who used the scented geraniums wherever possible, would plant them in the protection of a wall or near the house, where the brushing of the leaves with the long Victorian clothes would create the most delicious fragrance. The scent is especially noticeable on a still evening after a July shower.

An Ideal Setting for Scented Pelargoniums: On a Stairway

Recently it was my great pleasure to enjoy the fragrance of these plants to the full in a small London flat, where numerous varieties were placed up the side of the stairs. The ladies of the house brushed the plants with the hem of their skirts whenever they passed up and down, creating the most pleasing, invigorating perfume which permeated right through the house.

Perhaps the most important of all the scented-leaved geraniums is *Pelargonium capitatum*, the essence of which is now used to replace the more expensive attar of roses in perfume. Another possessing the scent of roses is *P. graveolens*, the variety Lady Plymouth having an additional charm in that its leaves are richly variegated.

One of the loveliest of them all is the pyramid-shaped *P. crispum variegatum*, which covers itself in a dense mass of small crimped cream-edged leaves which retain their colour and freshness for years; they are deliciously lemon scented. Besides the enormous range of scents emitted by their leaves, the fact that these scents are pungent rather than sweet is a great point in their favour, for indoors a too sweet perfume tends to become sickly and monotonous, but one never tires of the pungent fragrance of nutmeg, sage, lemons and peppermint. But it is better not to mix perfumes indoors unless they be similar. For instance, the lemon-scented *P. crispum variegatum* is an excellent companion to the *P. crispum minor*, covered in small curled leaves, which carry the pungent scent of verbena. But to place either of these plants side by side with the peppermint scented *P. tomentosum* is to kill much of the fragrance of both.

P. tomentosum is unique in that its leaves are thick and velvety and are joined to the main plant by thin long stems giving it a most exotic appearance. It can be used to make peppermint jelly and for peppermint flavouring. This variety makes a good companion to the eucalyptus scented *P. clorinda*, a variety which will bear during midsummer a bloom of deep orange-pink shade quite the equal in size and quality to the best of the show pelargoniums. The only other scented-leaved variety to equal this in quality of bloom is Moore's Victory, which bears a rich scarlet flower and whose foliage carries the not too pleasant aroma of pepper.

For pot-pourri, the small leaves of the *crispum* varieties (there is also *P. crispum major*, which is also richly lemon scented) are the most suitable and retain their perfume for some considerable time. Just remove one or two of the lower leaves so as not to disturb the balance of the plant.

The oak-leaved geraniums carry a rich pungent scent difficult to describe. To some the scent is of incense, to others it is reminiscent of southernwood. It matters little, for the perfume is rich and pleasant, just right for a warm room on a dark winter evening, whilst the leaves are richly coloured and edged with gold. The original oak-leaved varieties are *P. quercifolium major* and *minor*.

In the same category of geraniums with a perfume difficult to define is the variety *P. fragrans*, which to some is pine-scented, while to others the leaves smell of nutmeg. An old variety having a definite nutmeg aroma is Lady Mary, listed in the comprehensive catalogue of Messrs Cannells in 1910; they suggest that the pungent *P. filicifolium*, with its interesting fern-like foliage is 'well adapted for bouquets and buttonholes'; it would be imagined more for its fern-like foliage than for its pungent smell, which would not seem quite suitable for a wedding. But for old churches, which so often smell musty, how valuable these fragrant geraniums would be, placed where their foliage could be brushed by the coats and dresses of those who come to worship. The lemon-scented *crispum* varieties would be most suitable, or the sweetly orange-scented Prince of Orange, which with the minimum of attention will keep fresh and retain its fragrance all the year round. This is an excellent variety for a window box, for it does not grow too tall; likewise the lime-scented *P. nervosum*, which today seems difficult to find in Britain. The slow growing Pretty Polly, whose foliage reminds one of almonds is another very suitable for a summer window box.

For planting in tubs or close to an entrance to a house several varieties will grow to a height of nearly 5 ft. and form dense, well-shaped bushes. In parts which enjoy a favourable climate, such as South Devon and Cornwall in Britain, the plants may be left in the open all the year round and may be planted into the open ground. Should the weather be unduly severe, the roots may be covered with bracken or straw and sacking. Those living in less fortunate parts would be advised to plant in tubs, to take these to a frost-proof place for the winter and spring and to keep the soil quite dry. Possibly the two most out-standing varieties for making specimen plants are Roll-isson's Unique, mentioned in *Sweet's Geraniaece* (1820), which bears strongly mint-scented leaves; and the equally old Scarlet Unique which bears foliage whose smell re-minds one of incense.

Frequently used for flavouring apple jelly in countries bordering the far shores of the Mediterranean is the apple-scented *P. odoratissimum*; it is so aromatic that but a single leaf is used in the preserving pan.

A variety slightly sage scented is *P. asperum*, which has

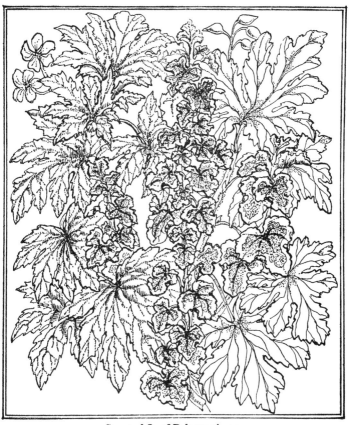

Scented-Leaf Pelargoniums
The basic fragrance is a blend of lemon, rose and balsamic scent.

attractive sharply serrated leaves. For mixing with bowls of summer flowers, sprigs and leaves of many varieties may be used, especially those of the more delicately perfumed varieties such as the almond-scented Pretty Polly or Little Gem; the rose-scented *P. capitalum*; and *P. radula rosea*, which makes a dwarf, bushy plant, ideal for the window box and hanging basket, and bears rich pink flowers. Like *capitatum*, the foliage is also used in the perfumery trade, for it is said to possess the scent of the old cabbage rose.

Two others with unusual perfume are Purple Unique, whose leaves possess the scent of absinthe; and *P. stenopelatum*, the only ivy-leaved geranium with fragrance. It bears bright crimson flowers in summer whilst its leaves carry the aroma of wormwood.

There are others; indeed varieties are being constantly re-discovered, perhaps growing neglected in the conservatories of old houses, or found in cottage gardens hiding their fragrance amidst a wilderness of bygone favourites.

Even a small collection will provide considerable interest, even if it is confined to the greenhouse where one may spend a pleasant hour when the sun is setting and the heat of the summer's day gradually giving way to the cool air of night, pressing the leaves; for they will not release their aromatic perfume unless pressed or brushed against.

Root them around the side of a pot containing a mixture of loam, sand and peat, where they remain until June. They may then be planted out for the summer or re-potted into larger pots into a compost containing some rotted manure; within twelve months of taking the cuttings they will have grown into large plants. But always remember to keep geraniums on the dry side, not too dry which will cause their leaves to fall, but if kept too moist they will turn yellow and lose their perfume.

More scented plants

The lemon-scented verbenas used in perfumery are now classified under *Aloysia* or *Lippia*, *L. citriodora*, a native of South America having leaves which smell powerfully of verbena. Of rapid growth, it will make a large bush 5 ft. tall and the same across in a single summer, but does best if planted against a sunny wall and in a poor soil. Even with this care, it may need to be cut down in a cold winter, but if ashes are heaped over the roots and about the base of the plant, new growth will appear again in spring. The leaves retain their lemon fragrance long after they are dried and a single leaf in a pot-pourri will add to its potency.

In a greenhouse or garden room, the plants will retain their bright green leaves, borne in whorls of three, all the year, but outdoors the leaves nearly always fall in winter, unless the climate is especially mild.

From Chile comes the strongly aromatic *Laurella aromatica*, a handsome evergreen shrub or small tree with leathery serrated leaves of brightest green. It is best grown in a small plant tub, like the bay laurel, *Laurus nobilis*, and lifted indoors in early November, where it remains until May, happy in the gentle warmth of an inner porch or entrance hall, or in a garden room. If wintered outdoors in a moderate climate, the plants must be covered with sacking. This will present no difficulty with the bay laurel, as it is usually grown on a long slender stem, with the head clipped into a ball or square. Or it may be grown as a pyramid on only a short stem. Native

There is nothing to compare with the allure and charm of
entering a greenhouse filled with a varied assortment of aromatic plants and enjoying the aromatic sweetness in the air.
Different impressions are created when the individual leaves are
brushed with the hand.

of South Europe, it was used by the Romans who crowned their poets and victorious warriors with wreaths made from the fragrant branches. The Elizabethans used the leaves for strewing and to include in pot-pourris as in Dorothea Roundell's celebrated sweet jar made up of half a pound of bay salt, a quarter pound of common salt, which was sprinkled over six basinsful of sweet scented rose petals, twenty-four bay leaves finely chopped, a handful of myrtle leaves, six of lavender, one of orange blossom and the same of clove-scented carnations. Stir the mixture each day for a week, then add half an ounce of cloves, four ounces of orris root (powdered), half an ounce of cinnamon and two nutmegs, all pounded. Keep closed up in a jar until it is required to perfume a room, then, after a few hours stir up the mixture and close it up again.

The dead leaves of bay burnt on a low fire will release their aromatic perfume into the room and fresh leaves placed in a warm bath will comfort tired limbs.

When planting in a tub, see that the base is provided with drainage holes over which are placed crocks. Then fill with fibrous turf loam to which a little decayed manure (or used hops) is added. Keep the roots moist in dry weather and do any clipping in early summer.

A little book called *The Toilet of Flora* by an anonymous writer of the early eighteenth century gives a recipe for using bay leaves to make a sweet smelling powder to place in muslin bags to include when filling pillows and cushions or to place amongst linen and clothes. To a pound of freshly gathered orange blossom (*Philadelphus*), one of sweet scented roses, half a pound of lavender flowers and a quarter pound each of sweet marjoram leaves and clove-scented pinks, add an ounce of fresh rosemary and thyme and half an ounce of bay leaves.

Place in a large pan and allow them to dry for almost the whole summer, stirring each day. The ingredients will dry completely and break up into a fine powder.

Sir Kenelm Digby (1669) also tells of the plants used by his friend, the Countess of Dorset to make a sweet washing water to add to a lukewarm bath. It is to take two handfuls each of rose petals, bay leaves, lavender, sweet marjoram, and clove-scented pinks; an ounce each of cinnamon and cloves. Pour over them two quarts of strong ale and allow to infuse for forty-eight hours. Then distill it and allow to stand for several weeks before using the aromatic water.

A deliciously fragrant annual herb which is rather too tender for cooler gardens, requiring a greenhouse or frame to raise the plants in spring, is sweet basil, *Ocymum basilicum,* native of India and the Far East where it is sacred to the gods Krishna and Vishnu. It grows in pots in most homes where it is worshipped by the household and this is how to grow it. Writing during Elizabethan times, Tusser said:

> Fine basil desireth it may be her lot,
> To grow as the gilliflower, trim in a pot.

And he said 'if the basil be stroked, it leaves a grateful smell on the hand'. Indeed it does, it has a spicy, clove-like smell and Gerard said, 'It taketh away sorrow which comes with melancholy, and makes a man merrie and glad.' Parkinson said that basil is 'in a manner wholly spent to make sweet or washing waters'. These are made by infusing a handful of leaves in hot water and straining. Then add to a bowl of lukewarm water to bathe the face.

It will keep through winter if the plants are cut away at soil level and strung up to dry (like sage) in an airy room.

Then remove the leaves from the stems and scatter in a pot-pourri. The finely ground leaves may also be taken as snuff, and with its camphor-like smell it will quickly clear the head when a cold proves troublesome.

The bush basil, Ocymum minimum is also half hardy. It grows short and bushy and all parts of it are pleasantly aromatic. Grow it in small pots in a sandy soil in the kitchen window and use the leaves as required.

The basils are raised from seed sown in gentle warmth in early March or in a closed frame early in April. Transplant the seedlings to small pots when they have grown large enough to handle and grow on until time to plant them out 12 in. apart early in June.

There is a variety of sweet basil called Dark Opal which has handsome bronze leaves which are also aromatic.

PART THREE

Further Practical Information

1. THE PROPAGATION OF AROMATICS

Aromatics from seed

There are many aromatics which may be raised from seed sown in the open ground in spring or in seed-boxes or pans; most will come reasonably true provided a reliable strain is obtained. Where it is required to propagate a particular variety, which may be grown for its variegated foliage or for the quality of its flowers or its habit, then it must be propagated by vegetative methods, i.e. from cuttings or by root division. Large numbers of plants may be raised from seed and cuttings to grow on in small pots for presents or perhaps to sell wholesale to garden shops for aromatics are such acommodating plants that they are now most popular for they will give a good account of themselves almost anywhere, in town gardens and in the poorest of soils. Plants may be sold in small pots in say, six different varieties and if neatly labelled, are sure of a welcome anywhere. A profitable spare-time occupation could well be the result.

If sowing in the open, first bring the seed bed to a fine tilth by incorporating some peat or leaf mould, and sow in shallow drills made with the back of a rake. Make the drills North to South and about 8 in. apart, to allow for hoeing between the rows. If the rows are covered with cloches, this will hasten germination. Do not sow if the ground is wet after rain; first wait until the soil is in a friable condition.

When ordering seed, make sure it is fresh, for old seed

will germinate unevenly. When the seedlings are about 2 in. tall, transplant to small pots or plastic trays divided into 1 in. cubes. From the trays the plants can be moved to small pots without disturbing the roots. Fill the trays with John Innes sowing compost, which should also be used for sowing seed in pans or boxes. The compost is obtainable from garden shops and must be freshly made so that it has not become contaminated by weed seeds and disease spores which may enter sterilised compost if allowed to stand too long.

Sow the seed thinly and just cover the compost. Give a gentle watering and cover with a sheet of glass to encourage germination. The container may be placed outdoors in a sunny place or in the kitchen window. Do not allow the compost to become dry and, as soon as the seedlings are large enough to handle, transplant them to trays or boxes to grow on for several weeks before planting out. Or the seedlings may be moved to small pots and grown on until they are about 6 in. high when they may be sold in their pots or given away.

Root division

Aromatics may be increased by root division. This ensures continuity of the variety, as does propagation by cuttings, and is the easiest method of all by which to increase one's stock. Not all aromatics can be propagated in this way; those plants like lavender and rosemary which grow from a woody stem or rootstock are difficult to divide and are best increased from cuttings. But balm, bergamot, the carpeting thymes, the mints and sweet marjoram will divide; this may be done either in spring or in autumn.

The method is to lift a root and to shake away surplus

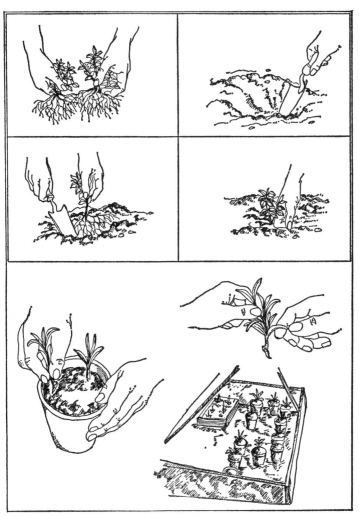

Propagation
Root division and cuttings.

soil. Then holding the root in both hands, 'tease' apart the numerous offsets. The pieces will come away with some roots attached and may be replanted in the open ground almost at once, or into small pots for growing on.

When planting herbs set them well down into the soil, for they will, in several instances, send up new shoots from below soil level. Always plant firmly and water in if the soil is dry.

Propagation by cuttings

All the hard wooded aromatics, i.e. lavender, rosemary, sage and the artemesias, the thymes and cotton lavender, are best propagated from cuttings. These are the small side growths or shoots which branch from the main stems. They should be removed by pulling them carefully away, together with a small section of the main stem; this is known as a 'heel' and the cuttings will root more quickly where this is present.

To encourage quick rooting, it is advisable to treat the base of the cutting with hormone powder before inserting into compost. The powder is best applied by means of a small piece of cotton wool made moist. Before treating, remove several of the lower leaves, so that the cuttings do not have to support more foliage than necessary; then, after applying the hormone powder to the base, plant them in boxes or pots of sterilised compost, or into a mixture of peat and sand which will also encourage rapid rooting. Keep them comfortably moist and shade from strong sunlight. As soon as rooting takes place, transfer the cuttings to individual pots containing a compost made up of fibrous loam, peat and sand in equal parts and grow on until the young plants have become bushy and are about 4 ins. tall. They will then be ready to plant out or to sell.

Cuttings may also be rooted in a cold frame, planting them 1 in. apart and into a similar compost. Keep the frame closed until rooting has taken place, and shade from strong sunlight.

The best time to take cuttings is during July and August, before the new shoots have become too hard, when they will become more difficult to root. The cuttings should be about 4 ins. long. Make them firm when planting by pressing the compost around the base. They will root more quickly if given a gentle syringe each day during warm weather.

2. HARVESTING, DRYING AND STORING AROMATICS

Harvesting

The harvesting and drying of scented leaves calls for great attention to detail. First, it is necessary for the foliage to have reached as perfect a condition as possible before removal, for only then will their full fragrance or flavour be released and retained for any length of time.

Much will depend upon the weather, for most aromatics are harvested, whether for their leaves or seeds, towards the end of summer or early in autumn, when the weather should be dry and sunny. A dry soil and a dry climate will ensure that the foliage (or seed) is rich in essential oil but, whatever the conditions, there will be a period in the life of each plant when it will have reached full maturity; afterwards it will begin to die back. If the plants are cut when damp, mildew may set in before they can be correctly dried, and the crop will rapidly deteriorate. Dryness from beginning to end is the secret of successful herb growing and harvesting. The plant must, therefore, be harvested before this happens and the correct time can be ascertained only by constant attention.

Those herbs which will be used fresh will, in most instances, require no harvesting. It is only those grown for their dried foliage or petals and for their seed which will demand care with their harvesting and drying.

Where the plants are growing under the conditions

they enjoy, it will generally be possible to make two harvestings, one in midsummer, the other in autumn. The early summer months, May and June, however, are often dry and sunny, and it may be advisable to harvest some foliage towards the end of June to make sure of at least one good crop. The shrubby thymes and the sages usually bear two crops.

Cutting the shrubby herbs, e.g. sage, savory and thyme, should be done with a large sharp knife, the stems being removed about 3in. above the base to prevent an excess of old wood from forming. When cutting savory and thyme, the whole plant may be held with one hand, while the cutting is done with the other hand, the sprigs being placed over sacking laid on the soil. Very hard-wooded plants such as southernwood or sage which have become 'leggy', will best be cut with a pair of secateurs to prevent undue pulling of the plant, which could loosen the roots. Soft-wooded plants may be cut with a pair of strong scissors. There are others, such as the mullein and tarragon, which will die down completely after flowering, and where it is required that the plants seed themselves the leaves should be removed for drying at the appropriate time and the flowers left to form seed. The stems should then be cut back, whilst annual and biennial plants are removed altogether.

Care must be exercised with the harvesting of those plants which are grown for their seeds, such as cumin, dill and coriander. While the seed should be fully ripe before harvesting, to allow the seed pods to open will result in the seed being scattered and lost. As they reach maturity, the pods or seed heads should be inspected daily and removed at the first signs of any seed shedding. The seed of annual plants to be used for propagating should receive similar attention, remembering that unripened seed will be devoid of keeping qualities and will not give satisfactory germination.

The seed heads should be removed only when quite dry, or here again mildew may occur. The heads should be cut and dropped into a cardboard box and removed at once to a dry room. There they should be placed in fine muslin bags and hung up to become thoroughly dry, after which the seed is separated by opening the pods over a fine riddle.

Drying

To dry the leaves of aromatics, the foliage should be left for an hour or so to become as dry as possible. Overexposure to the hot rays of the sun, however, should not be allowed or the flavour of the herbs will tend to lose strength. When drying on a large scale either for commercial sale or for home use, a small especially constructed drying room will be a decided acquisition. This should be built of wood with suitable ventilation in or near the roof to permit the escape of moisture given off by the drying herbs. A small aperture at either end of the shed or a cowl fixed in the roof will prove efficient for if excess moisture cannot escape, efficient drying will not take place and the herbs will become mildewed and musty. Shelves should be made of laths with a 1 in. space between each. Where small leaves are being dried, lengths of muslin or hessian should be placed over the laths. Roof windows may be used or windows let into the sides of the shed to enable the dryer to carry out the operation with ease, whilst they will provide a circulation of fresh air. Vents made just above ground level will also ensure an efficient intake of fresh air which will pass through the herbs and leave the house by the top vents.

Aromatic herbs may be dried in the home either by tying into bunches and suspending from the roof of a dry shed or room, (an attic is an ideal place), or they may be spread out on shelves or on trays away from the direct rays of the sun. Wherever they are drying, they should be turned daily so that fresh air reaches all parts of the leaves. The drying should be completed as quickly as possible, for only in this way will the aromatics retain their full colour and the maximum of fragrance. Especially is rapid drying necessary with those thick-leaved herbs whose leaves contain a large amount of moisture; mildew will set in if drying proceeds slowly. An attic or shed should be selected if possible, for the heat of the sun on the roof will enable quite high temperatures to be maintained, a temperature of $100°F$ ($39°C$) not being considered excessive where drying mint and parsley.

A rack for drying herbs may be made by using a number of trays about 4 ft. square. To each tray is tacked a square of hessian canvas, and the finished trays are held in position one above another. About 12 in. should be allowed between each tray to enable the aromatics to be turned and a free circulation of fresh air to reach them. A rack just over 6 ft. high may be inexpensively made and will contain six trays, thus enabling a large number of herbs to be dried.

Where space is limited and only a small number of herbs are to be dried, trays of similar construction should be made. These should stand on pieces of 2 in. timber fastened at each corner of the tray. This will keep the hessian 2 ins. above the shelving and permit fresh air to circulate around the herbs. This is vitally important, for rapid drying. It should be said that the drying room should not be made of stone nor of corrugated iron, for both materials tend to form condensation which will greatly hamper the drying. Where there is neither attic nor shed available, the airing cupboard will prove suitable and especially where there is a cylinder to which is fitted an immersion heater to maintain warmth. The door of the room or cupboard should be left open to allow any moisture to escape.

Storing

Where there is sufficient heat, most aromatics will have dried within a week. Where the herbs have to depend upon the natural warmth of the atmosphere, they may take up to three weeks to become thoroughly dry, at which point they should 'crackle' and snap to the touch. The leaves (or flowers) may then be rubbed from the stems between the palms of the hands, after which all unwanted material is removed. The dried leaves are then placed in a fine-meshed riddle so that soil, dust and chaff may be removed. Screw-topped air-tight glass jars may be used where small quantities of herbs are grown for home use, each jar being carefully labelled and placed on a shelf away from the sun. When storing larger quantities, possibly for sale, a large container will be necessary. Wooden drums are ideal for the purpose, for wood will not absorb moisture from the atmosphere. For this reason tins of any description should never be used, for they may cause the herbs to become damp. The herbs should be kept in a dry room, away from the direct rays of the sun and they may be mixed as required for use in many ways in the home.

Index

Books in the Living with Herbs Series

An open-end series of beautiful paperbacks you can use in so many practical ways — written by leading herbalists and herb marketers. Each book contains four pages of full-color illustration, and many black and white drawings. Each volume is $2.50 per copy and they also come packaged in a 4-volume set ($10.00) for holiday gifts. Four titles in print now, with more to come.

At your nearest book, herbal supply or health store, or order direct from the publisher (postpaid).

Vol. 1 Herbs, Health and Astrology
by Leon Petulengro

A famous gypsy and noted astrologer records some of the ancient Romany beliefs about herbs and their links with astrology. Health patterns found in each of the Signs are discussed and the author offers specific remedies for various ailments based on *herbal astrological confluence*. Mr. Petulengro devotes an entire chapter to each Zodiac sign and a description of how the planets rule herbs. Includes many unusual recipes. $2.50

Vol. 2 Choosing, Planting and Cultivating Herbs
by Philippa Back

Herbs for city and country dweller, for gardeners who plan whole herb gardens and for those who may want to grow herbs in more modest surroundings — in window boxes, on balconies, in pots hung on trellises, or for other indoor pleasure. Philippa Back co-authored the famed *Herbs for Health* with Claire Loewenfeld. She includes an alphabetical listing of herbs as well as many garden plans and herb drawings. $2.50

Vol. 3 Growing Herbs as Aromatics
by Roy Genders

Here is told the history of pomanders, potpourris, scented waters, hanging baskets, rose perfumes and other uses of aromatics and spices. Best of all, the author shows how they can be grown and harvested, and includes a variety of ideas and recipes for their use today. Roy Genders' books include *A History of Scent*, *The Cottage Guide*, and *Scented Wild Flowers of Britain*. $2.50

Vol. 4 Making Things with Herbs
by Elizabeth Walker

Professional help for using herbs to make gifts, practical and frivolous, to adorn and embellish the house. Sachets, sweet bags, herbal teas, herbal essences, herb sacks for the kitchen, toys stuffed with herbs, and all kinds of other delights become so easy with Ms. Walker's practical expert advice. The author's experience comes from running a very active family business called "Meadow Herbs" in England, which makes and markets herb products. $2.50

The *Living with Herbs* Series is published by
Keats Publishing, Inc., New Canaan, Connecticut, 06840.